A Robbie Reader

Gardening For Kids

Design Your Own Butterfly Garden

**Susan Sales Harkins
and William H. Harkins**

Mitchell Lane
PUBLISHERS

P.O. Box 196
Hockessin, Delaware 19707
Visit us on the web: www.mitchelllane.com
Comments? email us: mitchelllane@mitchelllane.com

Mitchell Lane PUBLISHERS

Gardening For Kids

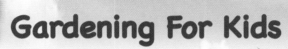

ABOUT THE AUTHORS: Susan and Bill Harkins live in central Kentucky, where they enjoy writing together for children. They have turned their entire backyard into a patchwork quilt of gardens, including a few gardens specifically designed to attract butterflies.

PUBLISHER'S NOTE: The facts on which the story in this book is based have been thoroughly researched. Documentation of such research can be found on page 46. While every possible effort has been made to ensure accuracy, the publisher will not assume liability for damages caused by inaccuracies in the data, and makes no warranty on the accuracy of the information contained herein.

Library of Congress Cataloging-in-Publication Data
Harkins, Susan Sales.
  Design your own butterfly garden / by Susan Sales Harkins and William H. Harkins.
      p. cm.—(Robbie reader. Gardening for kids)
  Includes bibliographical references and index.
  ISBN 978-1-58415-638-3 (library bound)
  1. Butterfly gardening—Juvenile literature.
  2. Butterfly gardens—Juvenile literature.
  I. Harkins, William H. II. Title. III. Series.
  QL544.6.H37 2008
  638'.5789—dc22
                                        2008002245

Printing   3 4 5 6 7 8 9

                  PLB / PLB2 / PLB2,46

Contents

Words in bold type can be found in the glossary.

Butterflies!

Many creatures will make their way into a backyard garden. Perhaps the most welcome are butterflies. They bring a garden alive with movement. Some are shy and elusive. Others are bold. Large ones float from flower to flower and then soar away into a **thicket**. Others bob up and down on a breeze, going where the wind takes them. With just a little effort, you can attract these delicate creatures into your space.

Even the smallest yard can find room for a butterfly garden. If you have no time for gardening, hang baskets of flowers or plant a few window boxes. Butterflies will even find their way to a pot of flowers on a high-rise terrace.

Planting the flowers that butterflies like is the key to attracting them. Keeping butterflies is another matter. They're not looking for only nectar. Butterflies need water and shelter. They need warm areas where they can bask in the sun. They also need the right plants for laying their eggs.

Before you grab a shovel and dig up your yard, there are two important steps you must take. First, get your parents' permission before you do anything. Second, get to know the butterflies and flowers that inhabit your area.

Butterflies belong to the insect world. They are in the Lepidoptera (leh-pih-DOP-tur-ah) order. Each species chooses a specific habitat. For instance, the rare atala lives in southeastern Florida, and the dainty Diana lives in the Appalachian Mountains. Don't expect to find either out of its habitat. Although butterflies are wild, many will adapt to your garden if you provide everything they need: sunlight; nectar from flowers; water; roosting spots to spend the night; and **host** plants for their eggs.

A butterfly begins life as an egg. Female butterflies lay their eggs on or near a specific plant, called a host plant. Without a host plant nearby, they will leave your garden to lay their eggs. Most host plants aren't flowers. In fact, the

Garden Tip

Butterflies are part of the food chain. Birds, wasps, and even spiders find most butterflies tasty. Some serious butterfly gardeners try to discourage birds, but it isn't likely that birds will eat enough of your butterflies to make a difference. Birds eat butterflies just as larvae eat host plants. This is part of the cycle of life. You can discourage it all you like, but chances are that you won't succeed. The birds will feast occasionally, no matter what you do.

Milkweed is a favorite host plant. Unfortunately, most gardeners treat milkweed like a weed—they pull it up and throw it out, eggs and all! When you find butterfly eggs on plants in your garden, don't destroy them! If the newly hatched caterpillar finds its favorite food in your yard, chances are it will stay in your yard.

most popular host plant is also one of the most unwelcome garden plants, the stinging nettle. Your parents might not want a patch of stinging nettles in their yard. They cause pain when you touch them.

Within ten days, a small caterpillar emerges from the egg. It is called a **larva**. Larvae come in a variety of shapes, colors, and sizes. Some are dark. Some have spines on their heads or stripes down their sides. Caterpillars live on and eat the host plant. As they devour the host plant, caterpillars grow, shedding their skin a number of times.

The swallowtail caterpillar can make a colorful addition to your garden. At this stage, it is called a larva.

Pupae on a birdbath. After caterpillars have shed several times (usually five), they hang upside down and attach themselves to a support. They molt one more time, revealing a gray bundle called a pupa.

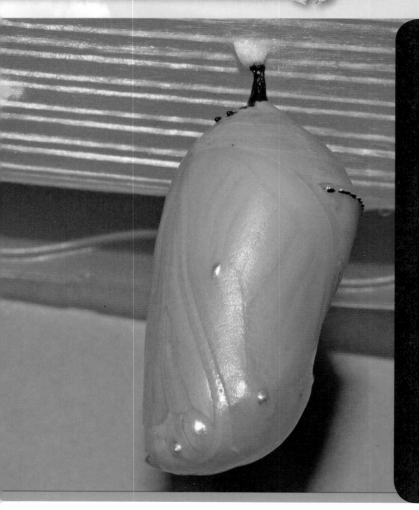

At the pupal stage, the butterfly seems to rest. It forms a chrysalis. You can't see what's happening inside the chrysalis, but big changes are taking place in there!

In about four weeks, the caterpillar hangs upside down or clings to a silken string. It turns into a **pupa** (PYOOH-puh). Then its skin splits to reveal the **chrysalis** (KRIS-uh-lis) underneath. This hard covering will protect the pupa as it turns into an adult. Like eggs and larvae, butterfly pupae come in many shapes, sizes, and colors. Some spend all

A monarch butterfly emerges from its chrysalis. You can see the distinctive chrysalis seal just below the top. After the butterfly emerges, it will need a safe place to dry its wings. It will hang with its wings down so that fluids can flow into them and the new adult can fly.

winter in their warm cocoons. Others emerge just a few weeks later.

An adult butterfly escapes from the chrysalis and goes in search of food, water, shelter, and host plants. If those things are in your garden, there's a good chance that the butterfly will live out its life there.

Chapter

Chapter **2**

Designing for Butterflies

Designing a butterfly garden is fun, and it isn't complicated. Pick a sunny spot and choose plants that are native to your area. Butterflies prefer large patches of flowers with a strong fragrance. Keep like flowers and colors together. Butterflies prefer pink and lavender flowers, in pastel shades.

Wildflowers are the easiest choice because butterflies prefer them to typical garden flowers such as roses and hydrangeas. Give butterflies a choice between a rose and clover (which most people consider a weed), and they'll pick the clover. Both butterflies and wildflowers prefer untended growth, which make them a great match.

Different wildflowers grow in different climates. Deciding which wildflowers to plant depends on your climate and the butterflies that live in your area. You'll find the best information on the butterflies and wildflowers that are **native** to your area at your county extension office.

After deciding which wildflowers grow best in your area, start designing your garden. Sit down and create a blueprint. You'll probably go through several designs before you're happy, but that's part of the fun.

You can purchase a mixture of seeds especially prepared to attract butterflies, but purchasing packets of individual seeds is a better idea. Planting a mixture of different seeds will produce a garden that looks like a bowl of fruity cereal. You might like it, but butterflies look for large patches of color that flow from one spot to another. Still, it's all right if an occasional pink flower makes its way into the lavender section and vice versa. In fact, that happens in nature.

Garden Tip

Your county's extension office will be listed in the government section of your local phone book. Most are listed as County Extension Office, Cooperative Extension Office, or County Cooperative Extension Office. It will have information on the wildflowers and butterflies in your area.

Providing water isn't a problem for most butterfly gardens as long as you plant wildflowers that are native to your region. Most of the time, normal rainfall is all they need. You might have to water your garden if you experience a **drought** (DROWT). Space need not be a problem. You can grow a butterfly garden along the edge of your property, beside your house, or along a driveway. All it needs is plenty of sunshine. If your parents aren't agreeable to the project, see if you can convince a science or biology teacher at your school to sponsor a garden on school property.

By far the most enticing plant is the butterfly bush (buddleia). Even a single bush will attract many butterflies. Put in a border of them and you won't need any other flowers at all. Butterfly weed is another favorite. Honeysuckle and daylilies are

If you can plant only one plant to attract butterflies to your garden, make it a buddleia. This "butterfly bush" comes in several shades of pink and lavender. Just one bush will attract dozens of butterflies to your yard.

two more favorites. All four grow throughout North America in meadows and thickets.

Vary the height of your flowers. The tiger swallowtail likes tall flowers, such as sunflowers. Other butterflies, such as sulphurs and skippers, stay close to the ground. Provide impatiens, marigolds, and sweet alyssum for these. A border of lavender, daisies, or bachelor's buttons is lovely with a smaller row of sweet alyssum or impatiens. A mass planting of sweet Williams, black-eyed Susans, and zinnias is attractive to butterflies and people. Plant the smaller flowers in front, where you can enjoy them.

Butterflies are attracted to scent as well as color. Honeysuckle, wallflower, and dame's rocket have luscious scents that both you and the butterflies will enjoy.

Choose flowers that bloom at different times. Once a butterfly finds its way into your garden, it will stay if there is a constant source of nectar. Flowers bloom at various times throughout the spring, summer, and fall. If you live in a warm area, plant flowers that bloom all year, like lantana. In the colder regions, lilac will attract butterflies to your garden in early spring. Early summer bloomers such as impatiens and bachelor's buttons (cornflowers) will keep them there. Then make sure you have a late bloomer, such as the butterfly bush. Cosmos and marigolds have a long blooming season and are easy to grow from seed. They are **annuals** (AN-yoo-ulz), so you must reseed in the fall or put in new plants in the spring. **Perennials** (puh-REN-ee-ulz) grow back on their own every year. Asters and primroses have many blooming seasons. Make sure your garden has something to offer all the time,

The meadow fritillary is easy to identify by its square-bottomed wings. It flies low to the ground and prefers black-eyed Susans and dandelions—but like most butterflies, it won't turn down a good meal.

All male tiger swallowtails are yellow-and-black. Females are blue-and-black, and darker. Swallowtails float on the breeze, high in the trees. Despite their size, they can be hard to spot.

so butterflies will stay. Purchase healthy perennials from a nursery or ask a friend who also gardens if they have any to spare.

Don't forget about host plants, such as stinging nettles. If you live on the edge of a field or meadow, you probably have stinging nettles nearby. Otherwise consider planting some in an out-of-the-way spot. Perhaps your parents will let you plant a few behind a shed, barn, or garage. If you don't have host plants in your yard, butterflies will visit but they won't stay. The easiest way to acquire a stinging nettle is to find one in an open field and transplant it. Be sure to wear heavy gloves, protective glasses, long pants, and a shirt with long sleeves to avoid getting the plant's oil on your skin.

Tall shrubs, vines, and even small trees provide shelter from the wind and rain. They needn't be right in the middle of your garden. The butterflies will find them if they're nearby. Fruit trees are an excellent windbreaker, and some butterflies feed on rotting fruit. Don't worry if you can't provide trees, a tall hedge, or even a thicket. They aren't necessary to attract butterflies, but they do make it easier to keep the butterflies in your garden.

Common Butterflies

Common Name	Latin Name	Range	Description	Host	Nectar
Black Swallowtail	*Paplio polyxenes*	Continental United States except West Coast	Black with yellow patches	Carrot, parsley, celery, dill	Butterfly weed, phlox, clover, thistle
Giant Swallowtail	*Papilio cresphontes*	Southern and eastern United States	Black above with patches of yellow, mostly yellow below	Citrus trees	Honeysuckle, azalea
Eastern Tiger Swallowtail	*Papilio glaucus*	Continental United States except West Coast	Black above with patches of metallic blue and orange spots	Spicebush, sassafras	Honeysuckle, lantana, azalea, butterfly weed
Checkered White	*Pontia protodice*	Continental United States except northwest	Mostly white above with black patches	Mustard, turnip, cabbage	Aster, butterfly weed
Cabbage White	Pieris *rapae*	Continental United States	Mostly white with black-tipped wings	Mustard, cabbage, broccoli	Lantana, impatiens, marigold
Clouded Sulphur	*Colias philodice*	Continental United States except coastal California, Texas, and Florida	Mostly yellow above with black margins and a black spot on each wing	Pea, clover	Aster, goldenrod, phlox, clover
Grey Hairstreak	*Strymon melinus*	Continental United States	Dark gray above and light gray below with orange spots on bottom wings	Hibiscus, clover, mallow, vetch	Goldenrod, milkweed, clover
Spring Azure	*Celastrina ladon*	Continental United States except for central and coastal Texas	Metallic blue above and gray below; color varies with season	Dogwood	Rockcress, buckeye, dandelion
Variegated Fritillary	*Euptoieta claudia*	Continental United States except west coast	Mostly dark orange with black lines and spots	Violets, passion vine	Butterfly weed, clover, shepherd's needle, milkweed
American Lady	*Vanessa virginiensis*	Continental United States	Mostly orange with black and white wing tips and blue spots	Pearly everlasting	Marigold, goldenrod, aster, butterfly bush
Painted Lady	*Vanessa cardui*	Continental United States	Mostly orange with black and white wing tips and black spots	Thistle	Aster, cosmos, thistle
Monarch	*Danaus plexippus*	Continental United States	Orange with black veins and borders	Milkweed	Milkweed, lantana, lilac, cosmos

Nectar Flowers

These flowers are shown on the following two pages.

Common Name	Latin Name	Color	Height	Sunlight	Zone	Flowering Season
Purple Coneflower	*Echinacea*	Purple	Tall	Full sun	3-10	Summer
Phlox	*Phlox*	Red, white, and blue	Ground cover	Full sun	All	Spring-Summer
Wisteria	*Wisteria*	Lavender	Vine	Full sun	5-10	Spring
Marigold	*Tagetes*	Orange	Ground cover	Full sun	All	Summer-Fall
Butterfly Bush	*Buddleia davidii*	Lavender, white	Tall bush	Full sun	5-9	Late Summer-Fall
Butterfly Weed	*Asclepias tuberose*	Orange	Tall	Full sun	3-10	Summer
Milkweed	*Asclepias syriaca*	Purplish-white	Tall	Full sun	3-10	Summer
Honeysuckle	*Lonicera*	Yellow	Vine	Full sun	3-9	Spring-Fall
Daylily	*Hemerocallis*	Various	Tall	Full sun	3-10	Spring-Fall
Sweet Alyssum	*Lobularia maritime*	White, pink, purple	Ground cover	Full sun	All	Year-round*
Astilbe	*Astilbe*	Pink	Tall	Partial shade	4-10	Summer
Lavender	*Lavandula*	Lavender	Tall	Full sun	8-10	Year-round*
Impatiens	*Impatiens*	Various	Ground cover	Full sun or partial shade	All	Summer
Sunflowers	*Helianthus*	Orange-yellow	Tall	Full sun	All	Summer-Fall
Lantana	*Lantana*	Various	Tall	Full sun	8-10	Year-round*
Wallflower	*Cheiranthus cheiri*	Orange	Tall	Full sun	8-10	Spring-Summer
Lilac	*Syringa vulgaris*	Lavender	Tall bush	Full sun	3-7	Spring
Cosmos	*Cosmos*	Various	Tall	Full sun	All	Summer-Fall
Aster	*Aster*	Various	Tall	Full sun	4-10	Summer-Fall
Zinnia	*Zinnia*	Various	Tall	Full sun	All	Summer-Fall
Cornflower (bachelor's button)	*Centaurea cyanus*	Various	Tall	Full sun	All	Summer

*Year-round in warm climates

Nectar Flowers

Purple coneflower

Phlox

Wisteria

Butterfly weed

Milkweed

Honeysuckle

Impatiens

Sunflowers

Lantana

Aster

Zinnia

Nectar Flowers

Marigold

Daylily

Butterfly bush

Sweet alyssum

Astilbe

Lavender

Wallflower

Lilac

Cosmos

Cornflower
(bachelor's button)

Preparing the Ground

Preparing the ground for some types of flower gardens can be expensive. Some tasks are better left to adults and even professionals. The good news is that butterflies prefer wild, untended land. Therefore butterfly gardens are easy to plant. Planning is the key.

With your blueprint in hand, stake out your garden. Hammer small stakes into the ground and then tie twine to the stakes to outline the garden's edge. Be prepared to change your plan if necessary.

Then remove the existing grass, weeds, and **debris** (duh-BREE) from your plot. A rototiller will come in handy if you have one. This gas-powered machine has blades that will cut through the dirt. **Ask an adult** to run the tiller for you. If you're outside while someone's tilling the ground, wear protective glasses. Tillers throw out rocks and other debris, just like lawn mowers do.

If you don't have a tiller, use a pointed **spade** to dig up the **sod** and weeds. Use the spade to cut small sections of the sod. Dig under each section, and then lift it up and shake off as much soil as you can. Shake soil off the roots of the weeds you pull up, too. Then throw the sod and weeds into a

When you clear your garden plot, you might have large branches to throw out. Break them into smaller pieces, and take them to your town's drop-off point for yard waste. Invite some friends over to join in the fun!

wheelbarrow or bucket. Collect them in one place. If it's okay with your parents, you can leave the pile in an unseen place. Or you can use small but strong garbage bags to dispose of the sod and weeds. If your town has a green waste program, put the bags on the curb for pickup, or ask your parents to help you take them to the city's drop-off bins.

While you work, be sure to wear shoes that protect your feet. Keep in mind that they'll get dirty. It's also a good idea to wear gardening gloves. They will protect you from pieces of glass or metal that you might turn up as you clear the ground. They'll also help prevent blisters.

If you have time to wait, let Mother Nature do the hard work. Cut or rip open the seams of several large garbage bags and spread them over the grass and weeds. Some will overlap, but that's all right. Place rocks on top of the bags to weigh them down. Then leave them for a few months until all of the plant life underneath is dead. The longer you leave the bags in place, the easier it will be to remove the dead growth. A great time to put them in place is early fall. By the time you are ready to start your garden in the spring, they will have done their job.

The spot left after an aboveground pool is removed is a perfect place to start a garden. There's nothing alive to dig up! If you're not going to plant

The last thing you must do before you plant is rake the loose dirt to make your garden as level as possible. Some flowers prefer small mounds, but create those after you level the ground.

anything right away, cover the area with landscaping cloth or plastic bags to stop weeds from growing.

Once the sod and weeds are cleared away, use a **hoe** to loosen the soil. Now is also a good time to add garden soil or manure, which will provide the **nutrients** (NOO-tree-unts) plants need. You can buy both at a garden store. Ask for advice from the people who work there. They'll have some great tips on how to prepare your soil for planting. If you have a compost heap, you can add some compost to the soil, too.

Once the ground is clear of grass and debris, and you've loosened the dirt and added nutrients, use a rake to level your garden. You don't want to pack the dirt; just level it out.

Garden Tip

*The same wildflowers that attract butterflies will also attract bees. That's good because bees **pollinate** flowers and keep the growing cycle going from year to year. If someone in your family is allergic to bee stings, put your butterfly garden at the farthest boundary of your property. Most bees are active during the bright hours of the day. They generally don't sting if you don't bother them.*

Adding a border to your garden will make it pretty and help keep grass from growing into it. You can use bricks, stones, old railroad ties, or plastic edging from the garden store. Put the border around the edge of your garden. If it's a large garden, you can add stepping stones, too.

Now you are ready to plant!

Chapter

Chapter

4

Planting and Maintaining

Planting seeds and seedlings is a lot of fun. You can purchase seeds from nurseries or order them through the mail. Be sure to purchase flowers that will grow well in your region.

If you have room, you can **germinate** (JER-mih-nayt) seeds inside. You can purchase special planting trays, lights, and soil. If you're watching your pennies, use egg cartons or milk jugs. Cut the top off the milk jug and discard it. Egg cartons require no extra work.

After putting down a layer of old newspaper (to make cleanup easier), fill the trays with potting soil from the garden store or with loose dirt from your garden. Drop a seed or two into each compartment (for egg cartons). If you're using milk jugs or other types of pots, you can sprinkle the seeds over the top of the soil mixture. Cover the seeds with a little dirt. Water the trays lightly.

Poke a few toothpicks or craft sticks in the dirt. Then loosely cover the tray with plastic wrap, using the sticks to create a tent. You're creating a little greenhouse, so put the trays in a warm spot that gets just a little light. About a week to ten days later, you'll see tiny green spouts. Remove

If you grow flowers from seedlings, be sure to "season" the new plants for a few weeks before planting them in your garden. Take them outside for a few hours at a time to get them used to the weather. Check them every day, and give them plenty of water.

the plastic and set the trays in a sunny window. Water them regularly, but don't overdo it. Feel the dirt. If it's dry, give them water. If it's moist, don't. Check every day because you don't want the plants to sit in dry dirt for too long.

In mid-spring, prepare your seedlings for the cooler weather outdoors. You'll know the time is right when the afternoons are warm enough to play outside in a light jacket. Put your trays outside for a few hours each day. Stretch this period by an hour every few days until the trays are outside most of the day. If the weather turns nasty or cold, don't put them out.

When you're ready to transplant, water the seedlings so that you can easily remove them from the trays. Don't turn them upside down and shake them out. Gently tug the stem where it protrudes from the dirt. Easy does it! Take as much dirt with the seedling as you can. Remember: You've been tending these flowers for several months. Don't be in a rush to plant them.

Set each flower's roots into a shallow hole in the garden and cover the roots with dirt. Use your fingers to tap dirt around the roots, but not too tightly. The plant should be secure enough to stand on its own, but don't worry if it leans just a little. Transplanting is stressful for most plants, and they often droop a bit for a few days. How closely you plant them depends on the flower. Refer to the instructions on the seed packet.

When you're done, use a sprinkler, watering can, or watering attachment for your hose to water the flowerbed. A soft, misty shower is best. Water

Purple coneflowers attract a variety of butterflies, including the cabbage white. On this common butterfly, the black wing tips and spots on the upper wings almost disappear when the wings are closed.

Garden Tip

In the fall, if you let the flowers die back naturally instead of cutting them down, wildflowers will reseed themselves. Even so, reseeding is still a good idea. Simply toss small handfuls of seeds into the patch sometime in November. If the patch is completely bare, cover the seeds with straw. Avoid using raked leaves and grass to cover your flower patch. Doing so can introduce weeds to your garden.

your flowers every day if necessary for the first few weeks. Check the soil. If it's dry, give them water. If it's moist, skip a day.

If the weather turns cold, you'll need to cover your flowers. Secure a few sticks in the ground and drape old sheets, tablecloths, or newspaper over them. This will protect them from frost. A hard frost could kill your plants.

You don't have to start your seeds inside. Wildflowers germinate well outside. The best time to sow wildflower seeds is in the fall. November is a good month. Sow the seeds before the first hard freeze. Just don't be in too big a hurry. You must wait until it's cold enough to keep the seeds from germinating. You can wait until spring to sow seeds outside, but you won't have flowers as early. Wait until after the season's last frost. If you live in the south where it seldom frosts, you can sow seeds most times of the year.

When the seedlings are about two inches tall, thin them. Each seedling should be about an inch from any other seedling. After that, Mother Nature will take care of the thinning for you.

Don't use **pesticides** (PES-tih-syds) to discourage weeds and insect pests. Anything that kills them will also kill butterflies and caterpillars. If you plant wildflowers that grow naturally in your area, you won't have too many pest problems. Those plants are already used to the climate and **indigenous** (in-DIH-jeh-nus) pests.

The number one goal is to enjoy your garden! Try to find a few favorite spots where you can sit still and observe. Wear a colorful hat or T-shirt to blend in. Just pretend you're a flower and wait. If something buzzes by your head, try not to swat at it—it might be a hummingbird!

When you first put your plants in the ground, you will need to keep your garden watered and weeded. Pull the weeds as soon as they sprout. Once your garden is in full bloom, you won't have to work as hard to keep it healthy.

Early on, when your wildflowers are beginning to sprout, it will be difficult to know the wildflowers from the weeds, which are simply wild plants that you don't want in your garden. If you know something is a weed, pull it up immediately. Be careful because some wildflower seedlings resemble weeds. The truth is, only the largest weeds impact a butterfly garden. Pull up the ones you can see and that disrupt the beauty of your garden. If you can't see it, don't worry about it. The wilder your garden, the better the butterflies will like it!

Chapter
Chapter

5

Butterfly Habits and Shelters

Most gardeners are content to provide flowers to attract butterflies. Once you have butterflies in your garden, it's easy to keep them there if they have a place to roost at night. Most will use trees and shrubs. A butterfly log pile provides protection for roosting and hibernating butterflies.

A log pile needs to be in the shade. Planting a few nectar and host plants around the pile will help attract butterflies to your shelter.

For hibernating butterflies, such as the mourning cloak, you can provide a hibernation house. You can buy one or build one. You'll need a rectangular wooden box with narrow vertical holes. The butterflies use those slits to enter and leave. Each opening should be just large enough for a butterfly holding its wings together to slip through. Place strips of bark inside for roosting. You don't need to purchase or build a house, though. Set clean empty coffee cans on their sides in bushes and trees. Cut long, narrow slits

All butterflies like to bask in the sun. They're cold-blooded and need the sun's warmth to fly.

in the plastic lids, and put them in shady spots. (If the house is in the sun, it will get too hot inside and the butterflies might die.)

Butterflies like to bask in the sun. They must have sunshine to fly because they're cold-blooded. Place a few flat rocks in a sunny but protected spot. Consider leaving a few open spots between your flowers for this purpose. If you're lucky enough to have an old tree stump, plant some nectar flowers around it. Place a few large flat rocks in your garden. Butterflies will even bask on a gravel or dirt path, especially if you line the path with their favorite flowers. Even a wooden fence post will do.

Butterflies don't need special equipment. In fact, the wilder your garden, the better. This tiger swallowtail is basking on a gravel driveway.

Before your flowers bloom, attract butterflies with slices of oranges and apples. A number of birds will also eat the fruit. Be careful, because fruit also attracts ants and bees.

Many butterflies, such as swallowtails, skippers, and sulphurs, get moisture and nutrients from the areas around puddles. In nature, you often see butterflies in the mud next to a stream or pond. To copy nature, create a shallow hole somewhere in your garden, but don't plant flowers there. Keep the spot damp. If it rains a lot, you won't need to do anything else—just keep an eye on your puddle. Don't let it go dry. Nothing bad will happen if it does, but the butterflies can't use it. Once a week, sprinkle a quarter teaspoon of salt around the puddle to attract them.

A variety of wildflowers and a birdbath will attract butterflies, hummingbirds, and other birds.

Whether you live in the country or in the heart of a city, if you plant flowers and provide water and shelter, you will attract wildlife, including butterflies.

 # Craft

Make a Butterfly Log Pile

A butterfly log pile is exactly what it sounds like. It's a pile of logs. The butterflies roost on and between the logs, and the structure provides protection.

You Will Need

- Several logs, three to five inches in diameter and three to six feet long (the thinner the logs, the more layers and pockets you can create)
- Plastic tarp or some type of roofing material
- Hammer
- Nails
- An adult to help you

Directions

1. Lay four to five logs parallel to one another on the ground, leaving a few inches between each.

2. Crisscross a second layer of logs on top of the first. Continue adding layers until the pile is a couple of feet high.

3. Cover the top of the pile with a plastic tarp or some type of roofing material. **Have an adult** help you nail it down so it's secure.

4. Pile one more layer of logs on top of the roofing material to **camouflage** (KAA-muh-flahj) it.

Craft

Butterfly Log Pile

Cover with tarp or roofing material (nailed down)

Add final layer of logs for camouflage

Cutaway view of roosting butterflies

Stack logs 3 feet to 5 feet tall

Place near nectar flowers or shrubs

Use logs 3 feet to 6 feet long

# Further Reading

Books

Allen, Thomas J. *Caterpillars in the Field and Garden: A Field Guide to the Butterfly*. Oxford, United Kingdom: Oxford University Press, 2005.

Burris, Judy. *The Life Cycles of Butterflies: From Egg to Maturity, a Visual Guide to 23 Common Garden Butterflies*. North Adams, Massachusetts: Storey Pub, 2006.

Diehn, Gwen, Terry Krautwurst, and Bobbe Needham. *Nature Smart: Awesome Projects to Make With Mother Nature's Help*. New York: Main Street, 2003.

Farndon, John. *Butterflies and Moths*. San Diego: Blackbirch Press, 2004.

Harcourt School Publishers Staff. *The Butterfly Garden*. Princeton, New Jersey: Harcourt School Publishers, 2002.

Hewitt, Sally. Local Wildlife: *What's in My Garden?* North Mankato, Minnesota: Stargazer Books, 2006.

Works Consulted

Dennis, John V., Nancy Arbuckle, Matthew Tekulsky, and Cedric Crocker, eds. *How to Attract Hummingbirds & Butterflies*. San Ramon, California: Ortho Books, 1991.

Grissell, Eric. *Insects and Gardens: In Pursuit of a Garden Ecology*. Portland, Oregon: Timber Press, 2001.

Lewis, Alcinda, ed. *Butterfly Gardens*. New York: Brooklyn Botanic Garden, Inc., 1996.

Nancarrow, Loren, and Janet Hogan Taylor. *Dead Daisies Make Me Crazy: Garden Solutions Without Chemical Pollution*. Berkeley, California: Ten Speed Press, 2000.

Schneck, Marcus. *Butterflies: How to Identify and Attract Them to Your Garden*. Emmaus, Pennsylvania: Rodale Press, 1990.

Schneck, Marcus. *Creating a Butterfly Garden*. London: Quarto Publishing, Inc., 1993.

Tekulsky, Mathew. *The Butterfly Garden: Turning Your Garden, Window Box, or Backyard into a Beautiful Home for Butterflies*. Boston: Harvard Common Press, 1985.

Warren, E.J.M. *The Country Diary Book of Creating a Butterfly Garden*. New York: Henry Holt and Company, 1988.

On the Internet

The Lepidopterists' Society
http://facweb.furman.edu/~snyderjohn/lepsoc/index1.htm

National Wildlife Federation; Create a Certified Wildlife Habitat
http://www.nwf.org/backyard/

The United States National Arboretum; USDA Plant Hardiness Zone Map
http://www.usna.usda.gov/Hardzone/ushzmap.html

The University of Texas at Austin; Lady Bird Johnson Wildflower Center
http://www.wildflower.org/

The Xerces Society
http://www.xerces.org/about.htm

 Glossary

annuals (AN-yoo-ulz)—Plants that live for only one year or season.

camouflage (KAA-muh-flahj)—The act of disguising something by making it blend with its surroundings.

chrysalis (KRIS-uh-lis)—The hard outer covering of a pupa as it turns into a butterfly or moth.

debris (duh-BREE)—Broken-down, discarded junk.

drought (DROWT)—A long period of very dry weather.

germinate (JER-mih-nayt)—To start to grow (as from a seed).

hoe (HOH)—A gardening utensil with a square edge for breaking up hard dirt.

host (HOHST)—A plant or animal on which another lives or feeds.

indigenous (in-DIH-juh-nus)—Native to a particular area or country.

larva (LAR-vuh)—A wingless often wormlike form such as a caterpillar that hatches from the egg of many insects. The plural is **larvae.**

native (NAY-tiv)—Occurs naturally in an area.

nutrients (NOO-tree-unts)—Chemicals that help things grow.

pesticides (PES-tih-sydz)—Toxic chemicals used to kill plants and insects.

perennials (puh-REN-ee-ulz)—Plants that live for several years.

pollinate (PAH-lih-nayt)—To move pollen from one plant to another.

pupa (PYOOH-puh)—An insect that is changing from a larva to an adult. The plural is **pupae.**

sod (SOD)—A layer of grass and roots.

spade (SPAYD)—A shovel with a pointed edge for breaking up hard dirt.

thicket (THIH-ket)—A thick patch of shrubs, underbrush, vines, or small trees.

 Index